CONTENTS

Interested in primary sources?

Look for this icon. Use a smartphone or tablet app to scan the QR code and explore more about climate change! You can find a list of URLs on the Resources page.

TIMELINE

2000 BCE: The Chinese first use coal as an energy source.

200 BCE: One of the first windmills is invented in Persia, which is present-day Iran.

1543 CE: Nicolaus Copernicus explains that the sun is at the center of our solar system and the earth orbits the sun.

1609: Johannes Kepler describes the motion of planets.

1750: Carbon dioxide in our atmosphere is 279 ppm.

1754: Joseph Black discovers carbon dioxide.

1774: Joseph Priestley discovers oxygen.

1781: The stagecoach is the worldwide standard for passenger travel.

2015: The International Panel on Climate Change meets to determine a path forward for climate policies and actions.

2014: Scientists record the hottest year since they began keeping track.

2014: Solar energy systems are located on more than 3,700 K–12 schools in the United States.

2013: *Solar Impulse*, the first airplane powered by solar energy, flies across the United States.

2013: Nearly 21.7 percent of electricity generated worldwide comes from renewable sources.

2011: The world's population reaches 7 billion people.

2010: The largest oil spill in the United States, from *Deepwater Horizon*, occurs in the Gulf of Mexico.

2009: Costa Rica declares it will be carbon neutral by 2020.

2007: The Green Jobs Act is implemented.

1999: The world's population reaches 6 billion people.

1998: CO_2 measurements in the atmosphere pass 350 ppm for the first time in human history.

1992: The Energy Star label is introduced to identify energy-efficient appliances.

1992: The Kyoto Protocol, an international treaty of countries committed to reducing greenhouse gas emissions, is adopted.

CLIMATE CHANGE

DISCOVER HOW IT IMPACTS SPACESHIP EARTH

Joshua Sneideman
and Erin Twamley

Illustrated by Mike Crosier

~ Latest titles in the *Build It Yourself* Series ~

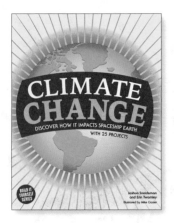

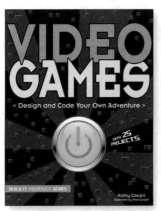

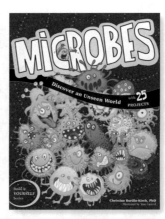

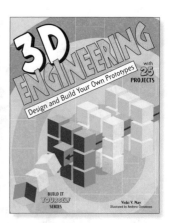

Check out more titles at www.nomadpress.net

Nomad Press
A division of Nomad Communications
10 9 8 7 6 5 4 3 2 1

This book was manufactured by Marquis Book Printing,
Montmagny Québec, Canada
April 2015, Job #112018

ISBN Softcover: 978-1-61930-273-0
ISBN Hardcover: 978-1-61930-269-3

Illustrations by Mike Crosier
Educational Consultant, Marla Conn

Questions regarding the ordering of this book should be addressed to
Nomad Press
2456 Christian St.
White River Junction, VT 05001
www.nomadpress.net

Printed in Canada.

TIMELINE

1800: Homes consume most of America's energy.

1817: The world's first bicycle, called Draisine, is invented in Germany.

1820: The term *greenhouse effect* is first used by Joseph Fourier.

1821: The first natural gas well is drilled in the United States.

1881: Coal-fired, steam-powered railway trains are the worldwide standard for passenger travel.

1882: The first hydroelectric dam is built by Thomas Edison near Niagra Falls in New York.

1883: The first solar cell is developed.

1890: The mass production of automobiles begins, creating a larger demand for gasoline.

1905: The first geothermal plant is developed in Italy.

1908: Henry Ford produces the Model T car.

1930: The world's population reaches 2 billion people.

1958: Scientists begin collecting data for carbon dioxide levels in our atmosphere in Mauna Loa, Hawaii.

1962: The largest producing geothermal field in the world is built in northern California.

1970: The first Earth Day is held in the United States on April 22.

1970: The Environmental Protection Agency (EPA) is created to implement federal laws that protect the environment.

1979: The first World Climate Conference is held.

1979: The first solar panels are installed on the White House.

1988: The Intergovernmental Panel on Climate Change is established as an international lead on assessing climate change.

1989: The *Exxon Valdez* oil spill dumps 38 million barrels of oil off Alaska's coast.

1991: The first offshore wind farm is built in Europe.

v

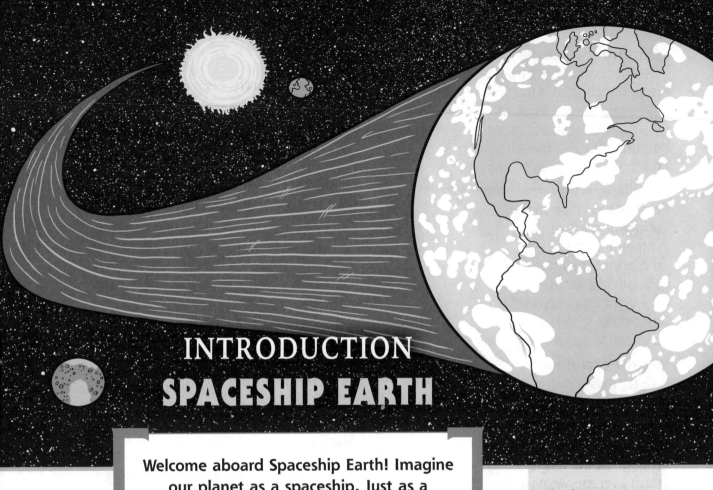

INTRODUCTION
SPACESHIP EARTH

Welcome aboard Spaceship Earth! Imagine our planet as a spaceship. Just as a spaceship carries everything its astronauts need to survive, our Spaceship Earth provides us with all the necessities for life.

When you watch a spaceship take off or look at photos of life inside a spacecraft, it's easy to see that the spaceship's **inhabitants** have to carry everything they need with them. There are no grocery stores or gas stations in space! Enough food, fuel, and water have to be brought on the spaceship for the duration of the flight. The ship also has **systems** to control both the temperature and the quality of the air, which have to be just right for the astronauts.

climate: the prevailing weather conditions of a region throughout the year, averaged over a series of years. These conditions include temperature, air pressure, humidity, precipitation, winds, sunshine, and cloudiness.

balance: when the different parts of something, such as in the environment or the climate, are distributed in the right amounts so that the whole system works and can keep working.

water cycle: the continuous movement of water from the earth to the clouds and back again.

climate change: a change in the long-term average weather patterns of a place.

atmosphere: the mixture of gases surrounding a planet.

WORDS2KNOW

By considering Earth as a spaceship, you can see how important it is to have freshwater to drink and clean air to breathe. It is our environment and our **climate** that make our home the way it is. Whether you live in hot, dry New Mexico or cool, rainy Oregon, you depend on the earth's systems to control the climate's delicate **balance**.

Most of the earth's systems are powered by the sun. The wind and **water cycles** bring rain that refills our freshwater sources while recycling the earth's fresh air supply. When the earth's systems become unbalanced, our planet experiences **climate change**.

COOL CONCEPT

The water cycle is the movement of water in a cycle between clouds, the land, oceans, and the **atmosphere**. A drop of water in the ocean may travel for more than 3,000 years before it falls as rain. Drops of water in the atmosphere may spend an average of eight days in the sky before falling back to the earth.

Metric Conversions

In the United States we use English measurements, but most scientists use metric measurements when performing experiments. To find the metric equivalents to the English measurements in this book, use the chart on page 118.

Climate change is the worldwide shift in the earth's normal weather patterns in response to human activity.

Have you noticed different weather patterns where you live? Have you heard about stronger, more frequent storms in the news? We experience climate change in many forms, from shorter winters and longer summers to changes in rainfall patterns and animal migration routes.

All of the earth's inhabitants have to **adapt** to the **impact** of climate change. Many scientists and citizens are working together to find solutions to our changing climate.

adapt: to change to survive in new or different conditions.

impact: an effect or influence.

WORDS **2** KNOW

natural resource: something found in nature that is useful to humans, such as water to drink, trees to burn, and fish to eat.

Take Care of Spaceship Earth

There are more than 7 billion people living on this planet using **natural resources** every day. We chop down trees for wood to build houses and burn for warmth. We use water to drink and bathe and wash dishes. We dig up gold and different metals to make jewelry, cars, and cell phones. How else do we affect the planet?

Earth Selfies

Astronauts and satellites have been taking selfies of Earth for years. Some show Earth within our **solar system** and others capture Earth within the **universe**. What do you see most often in these pictures?

solar system: the collection of eight planets, moons, and other **celestial bodies** that **orbit** the sun.

celestial body: a star, planet, moon, or object in the sky.

orbit: a repeating path that circles around something else.

universe: everything that exists, everywhere.

nonrenewable: resources that can be used up, that we can't make more of, such as oil.

oxygen: a gas in the atmosphere that people and animals need to breathe to stay alive.

WORDS2KNOW

We also throw a lot of things away. From food and toys to packaging and clothes, we all produce waste. Americans produce an average of more than 4 pounds of waste a day. If you collected all the garbage produced in America during one year, you could fill up a line of garbage trucks all the way to the moon!

The more people on the planet, the more resources we use. But many of these resources are **nonrenewable** and will eventually run out. That is why it is very important we use our resources wisely. Our individual choices have an impact on the entire world.

Spaceship Earth's atmosphere surrounds our planet like a blanket. It gives us the **oxygen** we breathe and sustains life by moving oxygen around the planet. The atmosphere also controls the temperature on the surface of the earth.

For thousands of years, people thought of "air" as a single substance. They didn't know it was actually a mixture of gases. Can you name something else that is a mixture?

COOL CONCEPT

Our atmosphere is composed of many gases, but the most important to us are nitrogen, oxygen, and carbon dioxide. The levels of these gases must remain balanced in order for our atmosphere to continue to support life.

Changes to our atmosphere can have enormous consequences, including global climate change.

Measuring Change

In 1958, scientists at the Mauna Loa Observatory began sending up balloons off the coast of Hawaii to measure the carbon dioxide levels in our atmosphere. More than 50 years of measurements have been graphed on what is called the Keeling Curve. The curve is named after American scientist Charles David Keeling.

5

GIANTS OF SCIENCE

Charles David Keeling

Scientists used to think the oceans **absorbed** all the extra carbon dioxide from the atmosphere, but Charles David Keeling (1928–2005) had other ideas. He began measuring carbon dioxide levels in 1958 from Mauna Loa because it is located at a high **altitude**, far from any continent. This helped make sure the air that was sampled was mixed. The tracking of air samples during a long period of time has proved that the amount of carbon dioxide in our atmosphere is increasing.

absorb: to soak up.

altitude: the height of land above the level of the sea. Also called *elevation*.

fossil fuels: coal, oil, and natural gas. These energy sources come from the **fossils** of plants and **microorganisms** that lived millions of years ago.

fossil: the remains or traces of ancient plants or animals left in rock.

microorganism: a living thing that is so small it can be seen only with a microscope. Also called a microbe.

WORDS2KNOW

Dr Keeling discovered a way to measure carbon dioxide in the atmosphere. The measurements on the curve named after him demonstrate that the levels of carbon dioxide in our atmosphere are increasing.

There are many different reasons for the increase in carbon dioxide in the atmosphere. Many human activities produce carbon dioxide, including burning fossil fuels and forests. All animals, including humans, release carbon dioxide into the atmosphere when they breathe.

This means a growing population creates more carbon dioxide.

Scientists study climate change by making observations, gathering **data** through **scientific inquiry**, and thinking creatively and critically about different **theories**. What impact do humans have on the environment? What happens when we damage it? How does this affect our climate? Scientists ask these questions, the same ones that we will look at in this book.

We need to take care of Earth, just as we'd take care of a spaceship, so that it can take care of us!

data: information, usually measured in the form of numbers, that can be processed by a computer.

scientific inquiry: an approach to teaching and learning science based on questions, experiments, and evaluation of data.

theory: an explanation of how or why something happens that is accepted to be true.

WORDS 2 KNOW

Good Science Practices

Every good scientist keeps a science journal! Scientists use the scientific method to keep their experiments organized. Choose a notebook to use as your science journal. As you read through this book and do the activities, keep track of your observations and record each step in a scientific method worksheet, like the one shown here.

Each chapter of this book begins with an essential question to help guide your exploration of climate change.

Question: What are we trying to find out? What problem are we trying to solve?

Research: What do other people think?

Hypothesis/Prediction: What do we think the answer will be?

Equipment: What supplies are we using?

Method: What procedure are we following?

Results: What happened and why?

? **ESSENTIAL QUESTION**

Keep the question in your mind as you read the chapter. At the end of each chapter, use your science journal to record your thoughts and answers.

OBSERVE AND RECORD THE WATER CYCLE

IDEAS FOR SUPPLIES
ice ∗ cooking pot ∗ timer ∗ thermometer

The water cycle plays a major role in our earth's climate. It both stores and transfers energy from the sun. In the water cycle, water changes from a solid to a liquid to a gas, back and forth, over and over again. Can you name some solids, liquids, and gases?

During the water cycle, bodies of water such as lakes and oceans absorb the sun's energy. Some of the water **evaporates**. When **water vapor** enters the atmosphere, it cools or **condenses** into droplets. During condensation, the droplets become clouds. When the water droplets become heavy enough, they fall as rain or snow, depending on the temperature. This is called **precipitation**. How do you think melting and freezing fits into the water cycle?

As you use the scientific method to make observations and collect data, trust your data and make observations without judgment. Your thermometer is not broken! **Caution: Ask an adult to supervise the boiling of water.**

evaporate: when a liquid heats up and changes into a gas.

water vapor: water as a gas, such as fog, steam, or mist.

WORDS 2 KNOW

condense: when a gas cools down and changes into a liquid.

precipitation: condensed water vapor that falls to the earth's surface in the form of rain, snow, sleet, or hail.

1 Create a data table in your science journal like the one on the next page. Use this table to record your observations and make connections to your own life experiences.

2 Start a scientific method worksheet like the one on page 7. Make a prediction for the temperature at which water will change from solid to liquid and from liquid to gas. This is your hypothesis.

8

	Prediction At what temperature do you think the phase change will occur?	Observation Actual temperature when phase change occurred.	Connection Where have you observed this change in your own life?
Solid			
Liquid			
Gas			

3 Fill a pot halfway with ice and set a timer for 3 minutes. Observe and record the temperature every 60 seconds. Be careful not to touch the bottom of the pot with the thermometer.

4 Place the pot on the stove over medium heat. Stir slowly. Don't heat the ice too quickly.

5 As you stir, continue to record temperature data every 60 seconds until 3 minutes after the water has reached a rolling boil. Once the water begins to boil, have an adult take over stirring. A liquid is at a rolling boil when it boils continuously, even when you are stirring it.

TRY THIS: Make a graph using your temperature data, with the temperature on the y axis and the time intervals on the x axis. What is a good title for your graph? When you connect the dots after plotting your temperature data points, do you see a pattern? Record these observations in your scientific method worksheet.

Ask your parents' permission to use these websites to create your own charts and graphs. Cover up neighboring QR codes to make sure you're scanning the right one! Why are charts and graphs easier to read?

BUILD A BALANCE BOARD

IDEAS FOR SUPPLIES
*round object such as a full soda can * flat object such as
a piece of wood * multiple objects to balance*

**Earth's atmosphere is in a delicate balance. Humans are
adding carbon dioxide at a rapid rate. The atmosphere
needs to stay in balance just like your balance board,
but it doesn't take much to create an imbalance.**

1 Try balancing your flat object on your round object. What happens?

2 Place similar objects on each side of
the board and try to balance them. Add
complexity by trying different objects on
different sides. What happens?

THINK ABOUT IT:

Was it easy or hard to balance
your objects? What happens
if you use a different round
object under the flat object?
What does this show you about
our atmosphere's
balancing act? What
happens if our
atmosphere is out
of balance?

CHAPTER 1
GOLDILOCKS AND THE THREE PLANETS

Remember the story of Goldilocks and the three bears? A little girl named Goldilocks sneaks into the bears' home and tries to find food that's not too hot and not too cold, a chair that's not too big and not too small, and a bed that's not too hard and not too soft. She is looking for things that are just right.

Scientists who study planets can relate to the story of Goldilocks as they explore the universe with their powerful telescopes, looking for places where life might exist. These planetary scientists examine whether a planet is too hot or too cold, too big or too small, and whether the atmosphere is too thin or too thick for life to exist. They are hoping to find planets where conditions are just right for liquid water to exist. Planetary scientists call these planets "Goldilocks planets."

? ESSENTIAL QUESTION

How do scientists know if a planet is a Goldilocks planet? What do they measure to find out?

If a planet orbits too closely to its sun, it will be too hot. If the planet orbits too far away, it will be too cold. The area where an orbit is just right is called the habitable zone. A planet in the habitable zone won't be too hot or too cold. It will be just right. Planets that are too small don't have enough gravity to maintain an atmosphere. They cool too quickly for life to exist. A planet that is too big, such as Jupiter, the largest planet in our solar system, has no land. It is made of mostly gas and ice.

Earth is a Goldilocks planet. Conditions are just right for water to exist as a solid, liquid, and gas. Astronauts have described the earth as the blue planet. Images from space show that nearly 71 percent of the planet is covered by bodies of water.

Should we call it planet Water instead of planet Earth?

habitable zone: the region at a distance from a star where liquid water is likely to exist.

rotation: turning around a fixed point.

elliptical: shaped like an ellipse, or an oval.

WORDS2KNOW

GIANTS OF SCIENCE

Johannes Kepler

How do we know about the orbits of planets? We can credit planetary scientists, including Johannes Kepler (1571–1630), who have observed planets and their rotation through telescopes. Before Kepler proved otherwise, people thought planets orbited the sun in perfect circles, but Kepler discovered that the orbits of planets are actually elliptical. NASA named the space telescope used to hunt planets after Kepler. The Kepler Space Telescope has discovered more than 1,000 planets since it was first launched in 2009.

All features of Venus, except one, are named after women. All features of Mars, except one, are named after men. All of the planets in our solar system, except Earth, are named after Roman gods and goddesses.

COOL CONCEPT

Hot Times on Venus

Get up before daylight or stay out after sunset and you can often see Venus in the sky. Venus is the brightest object in the night sky after the moon. It looks like a bright, yellowish star. Venus is the

second-closest planet to the sun, after Mercury, and the hottest planet in our solar system. How hot is Venus? Even metal will melt on this planet!

Some people think Venus is extremely hot because of its proximity to the sun, but the real reason Venus is so hot is its super-thick atmosphere.

Venus is covered in clouds so thick that almost no heat escapes back to space. The **heat-trapping gas** carbon dioxide makes up 96 percent of Venus's atmosphere.

WORDS 2 KNOW

heat-trapping gas: a gas, such as carbon dioxide, water vapor, or **methane**, that absorbs and stores heat.

methane: a **greenhouse gas** that is colorless and odorless, composed of carbon and hydrogen.

greenhouse gas: a gas in the atmosphere that traps heat. We need some greenhouse gases, but too many trap too much heat.

wavelength: the distance from crest to crest in a series of waves.

infrared: an invisible type of light with a longer wavelength than visible light, which can also be felt as heat.

greenhouse effect: when gases in the atmosphere permit sunlight to pass through but then trap heat, causing the warming of the earth's environment.

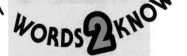

Have you ever gotten into a car that has been parked in the sun on a summer day? What's it like inside?

Sunlight enters through the glass windows and heats up the surface of the materials in the car, such as the seats and dashboard. Heat can't pass through the glass as easily as light because it vibrates at a different **wavelength**. The heat's waves are **infrared**. The air inside the car gets hotter and hotter, and when you open the door to the car several hours after leaving it, you encounter very high heat!

Venus is just like the car. Light gets in, heats the surface of the planet, and the heat can't get back out again.

GIANTS OF SCIENCE

Carl Sagan

Planetary scientist Carl Sagan (1934–1996) was the first scientist to correctly explain the mystery of the high temperatures of Venus as a massive **greenhouse effect**. Sagan fell in love with astronomy as a child when he learned that every star in the night sky was a distant sun. He helped NASA's *Apollo 11* astronauts before their flights to the moon, and helped design NASA's *Mariner*, *Viking*, *Voyager*, and *Galileo* missions.

The heat has nowhere to go because the atmosphere, like the glass windows of a car, won't allow the heat to escape. The carbon dioxide in Venus's atmosphere prevents the heat from leaving the planet. This is known as the greenhouse effect. We are experiencing a similar effect on Earth. As the amount of carbon dioxide increases in the earth's atmosphere, more heat gets trapped at the surface and the temperature of the planet rises. This contributes to the earth's changing climate.

Here on Earth, people use greenhouses to grow food, especially during the winter. Why do you think this works?

Scientists describe the extreme temperature of Venus as a "runaway greenhouse effect." They say it is running away because the atmosphere heats up to such a high degree that it never cools down again.

Extreme Living

Extremophiles are small **organisms** that can live in some of the most extreme conditions. They live where most humans cannot go. Extremophiles can be found in the super-heated waters of the ocean floor near heat vents, in the extreme saltiness of the Dead Sea, in the freezing cold of Antarctica, and even in the driest deserts on the planet. They provide us with clues that life may survive in some of the most unexpected places. Maybe even on the super-heated surface of Venus!

organism: any living thing, such as a plant or animal.

WORDS 2 KNOW

The super-hot temperatures and thick clouds on Venus make it hard for scientists to study its surface. The planet remains little explored and hidden in mystery. In 1982, an unmanned Russian spacecraft landed on Venus and sent some beautiful color images back to Earth. About two hours after landing on the surface, the spacecraft was destroyed by the extreme heat.

Is Venus a Goldilocks planet? Is it just right?

Cold Times on Mars

Scientists know more about Mars, which is sometimes called the red planet because of its reddish color, than they do about Venus. In fact, scientists know more about the surface of Mars than we do about the floors of our very own oceans!

The atmosphere of Mars is very thin, and this is part of the reason we know so much about this planet. It allows us to clearly see the surface. We use telescopes and rovers, which are car-sized, remote-controlled space exploration vehicles, to collect data and take pictures on the surfaces of planets.

The thin atmosphere of the planet also affects the temperature of Mars. Light from the sun enters the atmosphere, bounces off the surface, and leaves, allowing very little time for the planet to warm up.

If Venus is like a car with its windows rolled up, Mars is more like a bicycle. Mars allows all of its heat to escape back into space. Is Mars a Goldilocks planet? Why or why not?

Planet	Average Surface Temperature
Mars	-80 degrees Fahrenheit (-62 degrees Celsius)
Earth	57.2 degrees Fahrenheit (14 degrees Celsius)
Venus	864 degrees Fahrenheit (462 degrees Celsius)

COOL CONCEPT

The moon has no atmosphere to trap heat from the sun, so the moon is one of the hottest places in the solar system during the day and one of the coldest at night.

GIANTS of SCIENCE

Colette Lohr

Colette Lohr is an engineer and strategic mission officer with NASA who helps operate the Mars rover *Curiosity*. Operating *Curiosity* is a big job, taking nearly 90 people a day to make sure it doesn't break down. Lohr established Women's Curiosity Day on June 26, 2014, to highlight the role of women in science. On this day, women took over almost all the rover support jobs.

element: a substance whose **atoms** are all the same. Examples include gold, oxygen, nitrogen, and carbon.

atom: the smallest particle of an element.

molecule: a group of atoms bound together to form a new substance. Examples include carbon dioxide (CO_2), one carbon atom and two oxygen atoms, and water (H_2O), two **hydrogen** atoms and one oxygen atom.

hydrogen: the simplest and most abundant element in the universe.

WORDS 2 KNOW

NASA has been exploring Mars since its first successful mission to Mars in 1964, when *Mariner 4* took 21 pictures of the surface. Since then, the United States has successfully launched 18 missions to Mars. NASA also uses rovers to take pictures, perform experiments, and collect data.

Earth—the Goldilocks Planet

If Goldilocks were choosing planets, she would choose Earth—its atmosphere is just right. Sunlight enters the atmosphere and generates heat, but the right balance of elements and molecules prevents all that heat from being trapped. Just enough escapes so that liquid water, and life, can exist on Earth. All of these characteristics help create a climate that can support life.

One way to think about atmosphere is by comparison. Venus's atmosphere is 100 times thicker than Earth's atmosphere, and 12,150 times thicker than Mars's. The thicker the atmosphere, the greater the number of heat-trapping molecules. Since Venus's atmosphere is very thick, Venus is a very hot planet.

Venus

As you'll read in the following chapters, there are plenty of things you can do to make sure the greenhouse effect does not run away on Earth. In the next chapter, we will explore how climate and life are connected to the sun.

Earth

Why does one planet in our solar system have an abundance of life while the others appear to have no life?

Mars

Consider the Essential Question

Write your thoughts about this chapter's Essential Question in your science journal, using information you've gathered from reading and knowledge you may already have. Share it with other students and friends. Did you all come up with the same answers? What is different? Do this for every chapter.

ESSENTIAL QUESTION

How do scientists know if a planet is a Goldilocks planet? What do they measure to find out?

IDEAS FOR SUPPLIES

ice water ❋ empty soda can ❋ saucepan ❋ oven mitts ❋ cooking tongs

Is an empty soda can really empty? It might not have any soda in it, but it is full of air. The earth's atmosphere pushes in all directions—it's inside the can pushing out and it's outside the can pushing in. The pressure pushing out is in balance with the pressure pushing in. What happens if we create a vacuum **inside the can, making the pressure on the outside greater than the pressure on the inside? Start a scientific method worksheet in your science journal.**

Caution: Have an adult help you with the hot can.

1 Fill a saucepan with ice water and set it aside.

2 Pour 1 tablespoon of water into an empty soda can. Use oven mitts and cooking tongs to heat the can on the stove. Boil the water until a cloud of steam escapes from the opening in the can.

3 Quickly flip the can upside down into the ice water saucepan. What happens?

THINK ABOUT IT: Why is compacting recyclables and other waste a good idea?

vacuum: a space that is empty.

recyclable: something that can be recycled by shredding, squashing, pulping, or melting to use the materials to create new products.

WORDS2KNOW

COOL CONCEPT

Earth's air pressure is 135 times greater than the air pressure on Mars. What would happen to the empty soda can on the surface of Venus or on the surface of Mars?

Use your imagination to travel to extreme planets!

1 Thinking about the differences between Venus, Mars, and Earth, draw yourself exploring each planet.

Below are some things to think about.

* What would someone wear to explore each planet?
* What special equipment would you need to survive?
* How long could someone stay?
* What color is each planet?

Carbon Dioxide on Your Planet

Earth, Mars, and Venus all have carbon dioxide in their atmospheres. Even though Mars and Venus both have about the same percent of carbon dioxide, they have very different temperatures. Why?

Planet	Carbon Dioxide	Oxygen	Nitrogen
Earth	less than 0.04 percent	21 percent	78 percent
Mars	95 percent	less than 1 percent	2.7 percent
Venus	96 percent	less than 1 percent	3.5 percent

MAKE A TELESCOPE

IDEAS FOR SUPPLIES

2 cardboard tubes (one should fit snugly inside the other) ✳ *2 magnifying glass lenses between 1 and 1½ inches in diameter (one should be larger than the other)*

A telescope is a **scientific instrument** that helps us see faraway objects such as planets and stars. Telescopes use a pair of special **lenses**. An objective lens collects light from a distant object. An eyepiece lens refocuses the light to allow you to see the object. Telescopes come in various sizes and with different lenses. You can create your own simple telescope to explore the moon.

1 Neatly tape the edges of the smaller magnifying glass lens to one end of the smaller cardboard tube. This will be your eyepiece.

scientific instrument: a tool or device used in science experiments.

lens: a clear, curved piece of glass or plastic that is used in eyeglasses, cameras, and telescopes to make things look clearer or bigger.

WORDS 2 KNOW

2 Neatly tape your larger lens to the end of the larger cardboard tube. This is your objective lens, which collects light from the object the telescope is pointed at and beams it to the eyepiece. It magnifies that light enough so your eye can see the object.

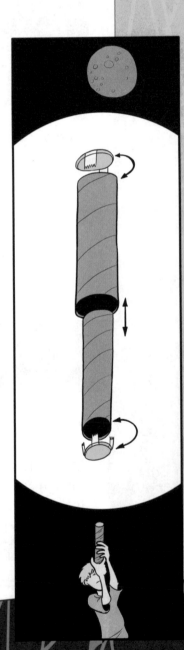

3 Try out your refracting telescope by pointing it at a piece of printed paper across the room. Adjust the cardboard tubes with one inside the other to change the focus. Can you make all the writing clear enough to read through your telescope?

4 Take your telescope outside at night and look at the moon. What can you see? With an adult's permission, find a map of the moon online so you can identify the areas you spot through your telescope. Draw your own map of the moon and label all the areas you can see with your telescope.

TRY THIS: Try finding star clusters in the sky. Research online to discover the names of these stars, and keep track of what you see in the nighttime sky in your science journal.

Exploring Mars

How do we know so much about Mars? Many rovers have been sent to Mars to study the surface and atmosphere. **Check out the video of _Curiosity_ and how it landed on Mars using new technology.**

To help explore how climate and atmosphere may be changing on Mars, NASA launched _MAVEN_ (Mars Atmospheric and Volatile Evolution) to explore Mars's atmosphere. _MAVEN_ is the first spacecraft mission dedicated to exploring the upper atmosphere of Mars. **Watch _MAVEN_ orbit Mars.**

BUILD A SOLAR COOKER

*empty pizza box * aluminum foil * black construction paper * newspaper*
*· clear plastic wrap * something to heat up, such as cold pizza*

Light from the sun can be used to cook food! A solar oven can be used to heat up a piece of pizza or make s'mores, but it won't get hot enough to burn you or bake things. Be sure to have an adult help you.

1 Make sure the pizza box is folded into its box shape and closed.

2 Trace the outline of a piece of notebook paper in the center of the box lid.

3 Carefully cut along three edges of the rectangle that you just traced on the lid of the box to form a flap of cardboard. Gently fold the flap back along the uncut edge to make a crease.

4 Wrap the inside of this flap with aluminum foil. Tape it on the outside to hold it firmly. Try to keep the tape from showing on the inside of the flap. The foil will help to reflect the sunlight into the box.

5 Open the box and place a piece of black construction paper on the bottom of the box. This will help your oven absorb the sun's heat.

6 Roll up newspaper into 1½-inch-thick rolls. Fit them around the inside edges of the box and secure with tape. This insulation will help hold in the sun's heat.

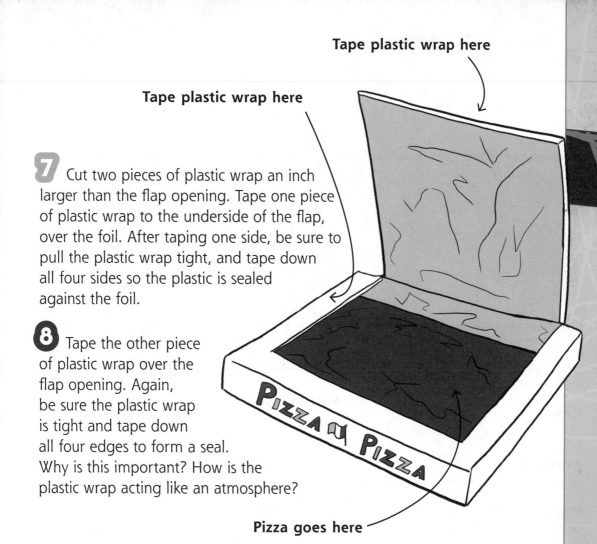

Tape plastic wrap here

Tape plastic wrap here

7 Cut two pieces of plastic wrap an inch larger than the flap opening. Tape one piece of plastic wrap to the underside of the flap, over the foil. After taping one side, be sure to pull the plastic wrap tight, and tape down all four sides so the plastic is sealed against the foil.

8 Tape the other piece of plastic wrap over the flap opening. Again, be sure the plastic wrap is tight and tape down all four edges to form a seal. Why is this important? How is the plastic wrap acting like an atmosphere?

Pizza goes here

9 Place a piece of cold pizza in the box in the sun. Open the flap and turn the box so the foil is facing the sun. Move the flap up and down and note how it reflects the sunlight.

10 Use a ruler or stick to prop up the flap so that it bounces the sunlight into the box, right on the pizza. Wait about a half hour for the box to warm up in the sun. Enjoy your warmed-up treat!

TAKE IT FURTHER: Can you use your solar oven if it is cold outside? Place a towel or blanket under the box so the bottom doesn't get cold. Set up the oven in the same way. Did your oven get just as hot as in the summer?

25

CHAPTER 2
BITING INTO THE SUN

What did you have for breakfast this morning? Eggs and toast? Cereal and orange juice? An apple with peanut butter? The sun is responsible for the energy in everything you ate for breakfast. This is because the sun is the primary source of energy in every ecosystem.

primary: the main source of something.

ecosystem: a community of living and nonliving things and their environment. Living things are plants, animals, and insects. Nonliving things are soil, rocks, and water.

food chain: a community of animals and plants where each is eaten by another higher up in the chain.

WORDS2KNOW

Did you have milk for breakfast? Milk comes from cows, and cows get their energy by eating grass and grain. Plants use sunlight to make sugar from carbon dioxide and water. This sugar, which is stored in the plant's cells, is the source of energy for almost all **food chains**. Most life, including the cow that made your milk, can trace the energy in their food back to the sun. When you bite into an apple, you are biting into the sun!

? ESSENTIAL QUESTION

How does the sun affect the earth? Could we have life without the sun?

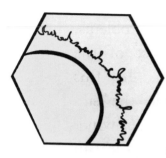

As you bite into your delicious apple, you have the sun to thank for the energy it provides your body. The sun's light powers all of the earth's systems. The sun gives us light and heat. Without it, the earth would be a cold, dark place that could not support life. Could the apple grow in deep space, where the sun doesn't shine and the temperature is -270 degrees Fahrenheit (-168 degrees Celsius)?

The sun's energy is trapped by gases in the atmosphere. This trapped energy remains in the earth's atmosphere, warming the planet.

Is the sun causing climate change? NASA scientists and satellites have been studying the sun for decades. Data collected shows that the sun's energy is released in a regular pattern. Since 1950, the sun's energy has not changed to have any impact on the increase of the earth's temperature.

So what is causing the earth to heat up? Scientists and citizens agree that humanity's demand for energy is causing climate change. We need energy for everything from growing food to building skyscrapers. For more than 100 years, we have been burning fossil fuels that release carbon dioxide into the atmosphere. This is what is causing **global warming**.

Do we need to burn fossil fuels? Could we tap into the power of the sun for the energy we need instead?

global warming: an increase in the average temperature of the earth's atmosphere.

WORDS 2 KNOW

renewable energy: a form of energy that doesn't get used up, including the energy of the sun and the wind.

biofuel: fuel made from living matter, such as plants.

mass: the amount of matter in an object.

WORDS 2 KNOW

The sun's energy may be one of the solutions to our climate change problems. The sun is responsible for most of the **renewable energy** on Earth. In this chapter, we will explore the role the sun plays in renewable energy, which includes wind, water, and **biofuels**. You will see how the sun drives the earth's systems, including climate, and is critical to life on Earth.

In one day the earth receives more energy from the sun than the world uses in one year!

What Is a Sun?

Our sun is a star that is 4.6 billion years old. It shares similarities with all the other stars in the night sky, except the sun is at the center of our solar system and the other stars are much farther away. This is why the sun looks so big when all the other stars look so small. The sun is our solar system's largest object, containing 99 percent of all its **mass**. In fact, 1.3 million Earths could fit into the sun!

COOL CONCEPT

Deep in the ocean where the sun never shines lives a type of organism that can make its own food without sunlight. These creatures, called chemosynthetic organisms, convert chemicals and heat into sugar. They get heat from vents in the floor of the ocean.

The Color of the Sun

Draw a picture of the sun. What color do you use? Although the sun appears to be yellow to the human eye, it's actually white. White is a mixture of all the colors of the rainbow. When light from the sun goes through our atmosphere, those colors are separated and scattered. Blue and violet light spreads out to make the color of the sky, while the yellows, oranges, and reds stick around to make the sun look yellow.

What is the sun made of? Very hot gases! The sun is mostly hydrogen gas (91 percent) and **helium** gas (8 percent). At the sun's **core**, hydrogen is **compressed**, which makes it very hot.

The temperature in the sun's core is more than 10 million degrees Fahrenheit (5,555,538 degrees Celsius). That is more than 12,000 times hotter than Venus! These high temperatures cause the hydrogen atoms to combine and form helium in a **nuclear reaction** known as **fusion**. Fusion is the source of the sun's energy.

More than 10,000,000 degrees Fahrenheit

helium: a light gas often used to fill balloons. It is the most abundant element after hydrogen.

core: the center of an object.

compress: to squeeze a material very tightly.

nuclear reaction: when atoms fuse together or split apart. This releases a large amount of energy.

fusion: when the **nucleus** of one atom combines with the nucleus of another atom, which releases energy.

nucleus: the center of an atom. Plural is nuclei.

29

How does energy from the sun reach the earth from more than 93 million miles away? The sun's energy travels in **electromagnetic waves**. The word *electromagnetic* means the waves are both electric and magnetic. They move continuously by pushing and pulling on electric and magnetic fields.

All electromagnetic waves travel at the **speed of light**, which is 186,000 miles per second (299,338 kilometers per second). That is the same as traveling around the equator of the earth 7.5 times in one second. Sunlight takes 8 minutes and 20 seconds to reach the earth at the speed of light.

If the sun were to magically disappear right now, how long would it take you to know it was gone?

Orbit and Tilt

The earth makes one complete trip around the sun every 365.25 days. This is called the earth's revolution, and it's how we measure a year. The earth's path around the sun, its orbit, is in the shape of an ellipse, or an oval.

Every four years we have a leap year. Leap years are when we add February 29th to the calendar. We do this because the earth's revolution around the sun takes a quarter day more than 365 days.

COOL CONCEPT

hemisphere: half of the earth. Above the equator is called the Northern Hemisphere and below is the Southern Hemisphere.

Scientists think of the earth as being divided in half at the equator, into two **hemispheres**. The top half is called the Northern Hemisphere and the bottom half is the Southern Hemisphere.

When it's winter in the Northern Hemisphere, it's summer in the Southern Hemisphere. That means when someone in Boston is having fun playing in the snow, someone in Australia is swimming at the beach. What causes the change in seasons, and why are the seasons different around the world?

GIANTS OF SCIENCE

Nicolaus Copernicus

Nicolaus Copernicus lived in Royal Prussia from 1473 to his death in 1543. His work changed how people viewed their place in our solar system. For thousands of years, humans believed the earth was the center of the universe and the sun and planets orbited the earth. In 1543, Copernicus published a book that explained the sun was in the center and the earth and planets rotated around the sun.

The earth does not rotate around the sun standing straight up. Instead, it's tilted on its **axis**. This 23.5-degree tilt of the earth is the reason for our changing seasons.

The Northern Hemisphere experiences summer when it is tilted toward the sun. The Northern Hemisphere's winter happens when it is tilted away from the sun. This movement around the sun causes a change in the amount and strength of the sunlight that reaches the surface of the planet.

In summer, the days are longer and the sunlight is more concentrated because you're tilted toward the sun. In the winter, the days are shorter and colder because the sun's rays are less concentrated.

PS

Having a Looooong Day?

Are days and nights always the same length? How many hours of daylight do you have in a day during the winter? During the summer? That number will depend on where you live. The closer you are to the equator, the less change there is in the amount of daylight. Enter your own location on this website to see a graph of changing hours of daylight for your area.

Sunspots

As early as 28 BCE, humans noticed dark spots on the sun. These sunspots can be seen through telescopes. The spots are actually cooler magnetic areas on the sun that appear in 11-year cycles. Sunspots help scientists study **trends** and patterns in space to better understand the solar system, from meteorites to temperature changes. Scientists on Earth who have compared the history of sunspots to temperature data on Earth have found that sunspots have been present in both cold and warm temperature time periods. This shows that there is no connection between sunspots and climate change on Earth.

Weather or Not?

Not only does the earth's relationship to the sun create our seasons, but the sun also impacts weather and climate.

trend: a particular direction or path.

drought: a long period of time without rain.

Weather is the conditions that occur during a few hours or days. We usually describe it based on amounts of sunlight, precipitation, and temperature. Climate can be described as the average weather during a period of more than 30 years.

If you live in Arizona, your climate is dry and hot. The weather may include thunderstorms or rain. When scientists study the trends and patterns in climate change they are looking at patterns across many years. These patterns can be found in temperature data or frequency of natural events such as thunderstorms and wildfires. Scientists say that climate change in Arizona will lead to increased temperatures, wildfires, and **drought**.

Can you guess the coldest place on Earth? If you guessed a spot in Antarctica you are right! Vostok Station holds the record with -128.6 degrees Fahrenheit (-89.2 degrees Celsius) in 1983 in July! Compare that to the hottest place on Earth, Death Valley, California, where a temperature of 134 degrees Fahrenheit (56.7 degrees Celsius) has been recorded. What is the temperature difference between these two locations?

COOL CONCEPT

photoelectric effect: the creation of an electric current after exposure to light.

solar power: energy from the sun converted to electricity.

WORDS 2 KNOW

Climate change affects different places in different ways. For example, the temperatures at the North Pole are rising faster than anywhere on Earth. The temperatures at the South Pole are not changing as fast. Mountain areas will be affected differently than coastal areas. Deserts will be impacted differently than rainforests.

No matter where you live, however, the earth as a whole is getting warmer.

GIANTS OF SCIENCE

Albert Einstein

Albert Einstein is one of the greatest scientists of all time. His 1905 discovery of the **photoelectric effect** was important for the development of solar panels. Without his discovery, we would not be able to produce **solar power**. In 1921, Einstein received a Nobel Prize in physics for this work.

Renewable Energy From the Sun

Renewable energy from the sun is all around us. Using renewable energy reduces the amount of carbon dioxide released in the air, and renewable energy technologies are less harmful to our environment. Renewable energy from the sun can be captured using **solar panels**.

The first home with solar panels in the United States was built in 1948 in Massachusetts by two women. Physicist Dr. Mária Telkes and architect Eleanor Raymond teamed up to build a house with a solar panel roof. This house proved that even in cold climates such as that in Massachusetts, the sun's energy can power a house. Dr. Telkes was known as the "Sun Queen" in the early twentieth century for all of her solar-powered inventions, including solar ovens and water-cleaning systems powered by the sun.

Element Symbols

Each element has a symbol, and when mixtures are made of those elements, their symbols tell us the number of atoms of each element in the mixture. This chart shows some common elements found in our atmosphere. Methane has one atom of carbon and four atoms of hydrogen. How many atoms of oxygen does carbon dioxide have?

Element	Symbol
nitrogen	N
oxygen	O
hydrogen	H
carbon	C
carbon dioxide	CO_2
methane	CH_4

dense: how tightly the matter in an object is packed.

atmospheric pressure: the weight of all the air pressing down on an area.

convection current: the movement of hot air rising and cold air sinking.

Renewable Energy From Wind, Water, and Plants

Have you ever been at the beach on a hot day and felt a cool breeze come off the ocean? You can thank the sun! The sun heats the air over land more quickly than it heats the air over the ocean. As the air over the land gets hot, it rises, because warm air rises and cold air sinks. Warm air is less **dense** and lighter than cold air.

The rising warm air leaves what's called low **atmospheric pressure**. The cooler air from over the ocean, where there's high atmospheric pressure, rushes in to try to balance the pressure. We feel this **convection current** as wind! If you've ever seen a windmill, you've seen the wind's energy captured to generate electricity.

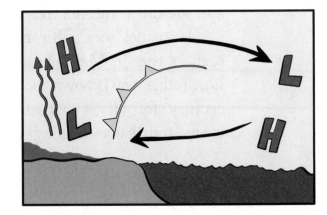

The first solar panels on the White House were installed under President Jimmy Carter in 1979.

COOL CONCEPT

The sun is also responsible for the power we generate from water. Energy from the sun warms the water, causing it to evaporate, turn into clouds, and come back to the earth as precipitation. This is the water cycle. Without the sun, rain and snow would not fall and rivers would not flow. Dams and other technologies convert the energy of water into electricity.

New Zealand generates more than 50 percent of its electricity from moving water.

Biofuels are another alternative energy source. Switch grass, sugar cane, sugar beets, **algae**, and more can be pressed into a liquid fuel. These biofuels can run our cars, trucks, planes, and boats. The U.S. military is the largest user of biofuel in the world.

The sun provides energy for plants to grow and the food animals eat. We can capture its energy to create heat and electricity for our homes and fuels for our cars. From the tiniest organisms to the largest animals, all life relies on the sun for survival.

Biting into the sun and using its clean renewable energy is our best chance for a cleaner atmosphere. Solar, wind, water, and wave energy can be converted into electricity without releasing a single molecule of carbon dioxide. Now that's clean! In the next chapter, we explore the balance of carbon dioxide and other gases in the atmosphere and the effect of this balance on the climate.

? ESSENTIAL QUESTION

Now it's time to consider and discuss the Essential Question:
How does the sun affect the earth? Could we have life without the sun?

BUILD YOUR OWN SUNDIAL

IDEAS FOR SUPPLIES
paper plate ✳ drawing materials ✳ plastic straw ✳ pushpins

How do you tell time? The oldest clock and first scientific instrument was a sundial. Created by Egyptians and used throughout history and even today in many parts of the world, sundials come in all shapes, sizes, and materials. Build your own sundial and mark the change in the sun's shadow to create a timepiece. For best results, do this project on a sunny day.

1 Punch a hole in the center of a paper plate. Don't make the hole bigger than the straw. You want the straw to fit snugly into the hole so it stands up straight.

2 Draw the number "12" on any edge of your plate. Draw a line from the number to the center hole. Use a ruler to keep the line straight!

3 At noon, stick your half straw into the hole in the plate and put the plate on the ground. Slowly turn the plate until the shadow of the straw falls on the line to number 12. Secure the sundial to the ground with some pushpins.

4 Where do you think the shadow of the straw will be at 1 p.m., 2 p.m., 3 p.m., and beyond? Draw a small X on the plate where you think the tip of the shadow will be.

5 Check the position of the shadow every hour and trace the outline of the shadow directly onto the plate. Write the number of the hour (1, 2, 3 . . .) on the plate at the end of the shadow. Continue doing this every hour until the sun sets.

6 If you choose, you can begin again in the same spot at sunrise and record the hours until noon to make a complete clock.

7 Write down your observations in your science journal. Why does the shadow seem to be moving? What object is actually moving?

TRY THIS: Research sundials online to see how other people have designed them. Can you find the largest one? How about the smallest? Oldest? How have sundials changed since ancient times?

COOL CONCEPT

The Greeks named the sun after their god of the sun, Helios. They believed Helios pulled the sun across the sky each day with his chariot.

HOW POWERFUL IS SUNLIGHT?

IDEAS FOR SUPPLIES
*dark-colored construction paper * various small toys or objects*

We know sunlight helps plants grow, evaporates water, and can burn our skin. We can even generate renewable energy from the sun using solar panels, wind turbines, and other technologies. What else can sunlight do? You need a sunny day to do this activity!

1 Put two pieces of paper directly in the sun at or around noon. Keep the other piece inside.

2 Place some toys on one of the pieces of paper in the sun and trace them with a pencil.

3 What do you think will happen to the paper? To the objects? Think about the heat and the light from the sun. Organize your predictions in your science journal using a chart such as the one below.

	Prediction	Observation After 45 Minutes
Paper in the sun		
Paper in the sun with toys		
Paper out of the sun		

4 After 45 minutes, compare the three pieces of construction paper. How are they different? How are they similar? What caused the differences? On a cloudy day, would it take longer to see any changes?

TRY THIS: Draw two pictures on two pieces of construction paper using ice cubes. Set one picture in the sun and the other inside for 30 minutes. What happens to the pictures? Why?

INVESTIGATE WEATHER VS. CLIMATE

IDEAS FOR SUPPLIES
drawing materials ∗ 7-day weather forecast

How is weather different from climate? Weather can be described as the day-to-day conditions. From a bright, sunny day to a snowy day, weather can change quickly. Climate, on the other hand, is made up of long-term weather patterns across many years. Let's explore some of the characteristics of weather.

1 Think of three characteristics of weather that might influence temperature, such as humidity, clouds, and wind. Read or watch the 7-day forecast from a few different sources.

2 Make your own predictions for the next seven days. Be sure to predict for the same hour of each day.

3 Collect data on the weather for one week at the same time of day for the same location. Use a data table like the one below to record your predictions and data.

Date	Prediction	Temperature	Characteristics of weather		

4 What did you learn about the weather? How did your predictions compare to your data? Were the 7-day forecasts correct? Why do forecasters often get the weather wrong?

IDEAS FOR SUPPLIES

handyman multimeter ✳ *AA (1.5 volt) or 9-volt battery* ✳ *apple* ✳ *copper nail*
✳ *zinc-plated nail* ✳ *2 alligator clips* ✳ *insulated wire with ends stripped*

How do we keep solar energy working at night? Batteries! We use batteries as a way of storing energy. Batteries create electricity from a chemical reaction. A piece of fruit, such as an apple, is an example of nature's battery. The sun's energy is stored in the fruit's sugars and starches. We can use those sugars and starches to create electricity. Start a scientific method worksheet in your science journal to organize, gather, and analyze your data. Practice using your multimeter with a working AA (1.5 volt) or 9-volt battery to ensure your circuit is properly wired.

starch: a type of **nutrient** found in certain foods, such as bread, potatoes, and rice.

nutrients: substances in food and soil that living things need to live and grow.

analyze: to study and examine.

WORDS**2**KNOW

1 Insert the copper and zinc nails into the apple, making sure they don't touch or go all the way through the fruit.

Handyman Multimeter

A handyman multimeter is a scientific instrument that measures volts. A volt is the unit used to measure the potential energy, sometimes called stored energy, between two spots in a circuit. The path of a circuit lets electricity flow when it is closed in a loop.

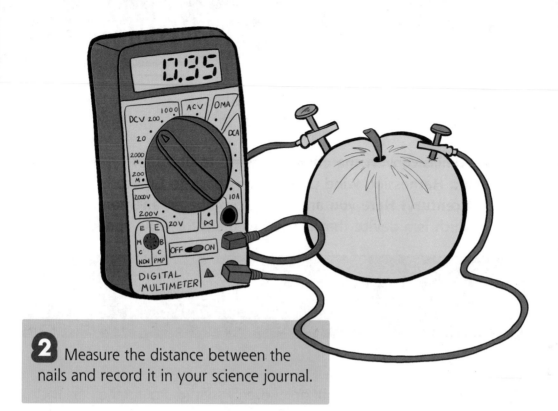

2 Measure the distance between the nails and record it in your science journal.

3 Connect the wire to both nails with alligator clips and check the multimeter. How many volts is your apple battery producing? Record your results.

4 What do you think will happen if you put the nails closer together or farther apart? Write your hypothesis in your journal and then move your nails to different distances and record the results. Does the electricity get stronger or weaker? Why?

TRY THIS: What will happen if the copper and zinc nails are inserted into the apple less or more deeply? What would happen if you change the size of the nails? Record your hypotheses and perform each test. Don't forget to record your results! You can also try using a lemon or potato for a battery. Do you think other fruits or vegetables will be better or worse than the apple?

IDEAS FOR SUPPLIES

5 paper cups ∗ paint ∗ thin wooden dowels or chopsticks ∗ empty water bottle

Windmills convert the energy in wind to do other types of work. Harnessing wind power dates back to Greece in the first century! Here you are going to make an anemometer, which is a device that is used to measure wind speed.

1 Take four paper cups and punch a single hole halfway down the side of each cup. Paint one cup a color different from the others.

2 On the fifth cup, make four holes evenly spaced around the rim. The first and third holes should be slightly closer to the rim than the second and fourth holes. Carefully punch one hole in the center of the bottom of this cup.

3 Slide two of the dowels through the holes in the fifth cup to make an X. Make sure the first four cups are all on their sides facing the same direction. Connect each through the hole in its side to an end of each of the dowels. Secure each cup to its dowel with tape. Why should they all be facing the same direction?